EUROPE

By Tracy Vonder Brink

A Crabtree Crown Book

School-to-Home Support for Caregivers and Teachers

This appealing book is designed to teach students about core subject areas. Students will build upon what they already know about the subject, and engage in topics that they want to learn more about. Here are a few guiding questions to help readers build their comprehensions skills. Possible answers appear here in red.

Before Reading:

What do I know about Europe?

- *I know Europe is a continent.*
- *I know soccer is played in Europe.*

What do I want to learn about this topic?

- *I want to know how many countries are in Europe.*
- *I want to learn about animals that live in Europe.*

During Reading:

I'm curious to know...

- *I'm curious to know what kind of foods Europeans eat.*
- *I'm curious to know how many Europeans live in cities.*

How is this like something I already know?

- *I know what foods people who live near me eat.*
- *I know whether I live in a city.*

After Reading:

What was the author trying to teach me?

- *The author was trying to teach me what kind of landforms Europe has.*
- *The author was trying to teach me about European countries.*

How did the photographs and captions help me understand more?

- *The photographs helped me picture Europe.*
- *The captions gave me extra information.*

TABLE OF CONTENTS

CHAPTER 1
GET TO KNOW EUROPE

What continent has ten major mountain ranges? Where do moose roam and hedgehogs burrow? Where do more than 700 million people live?

Europe!

Europe is north of the **equator**. It is part of a landmass known as Eurasia, where the lands of both Europe and Asia connect. The Ural Mountains separate Europe from Asia. Europe is a large **peninsula**.

The world has seven continents. Europe is the second smallest.

PENINSULAS, OCEANS, AND ISLANDS

Other peninsulas stick out from the larger European peninsula. Norway, Sweden, and Denmark are peninsulas in northern Europe. Together, they are known as Scandinavia. Italy is a peninsula in southern Europe. The Arctic Ocean **borders** Europe's north, and the Atlantic Ocean washes up against its west. Several seas, including the Mediterranean Sea, lie to its south.

Iceland is known for its volcanoes. A brand new volcano erupted in Iceland in March, 2021.

Island nations make up part of Europe. The United Kingdom includes England, Scotland, Wales, and Northern Ireland. More than 68 million people live in the United Kingdom. Cyprus is an island nation in the Mediterranean Sea. Iceland is in the North Atlantic Ocean. Fewer than 400,000 people live there.

CHAPTER 2

LANDFORMS AND CLIMATE

Europe has tall mountains and rugged highlands. Flat **plains** cover large areas of land. Unlike the other continents, Europe has no deserts.

The Alps formed about 44 million years ago. Snow became glaciers in the highest areas. Today, the Alps have about 4,000 glaciers.

MOUNTAINS

The Pyrenees Mountains divide France and Spain. Shorter mountains called highlands are found on the western edges of Europe. The Alps mountain range stretches through eight countries in central Europe.

THE EUROPEAN PLAINS

Low, flat plains make up more than half of Europe. The European Plains cover northern Europe, including parts of 10 countries. The European Plains extend from the Pyrenees Mountains in Spain and France to the Ural Mountains in Russia.

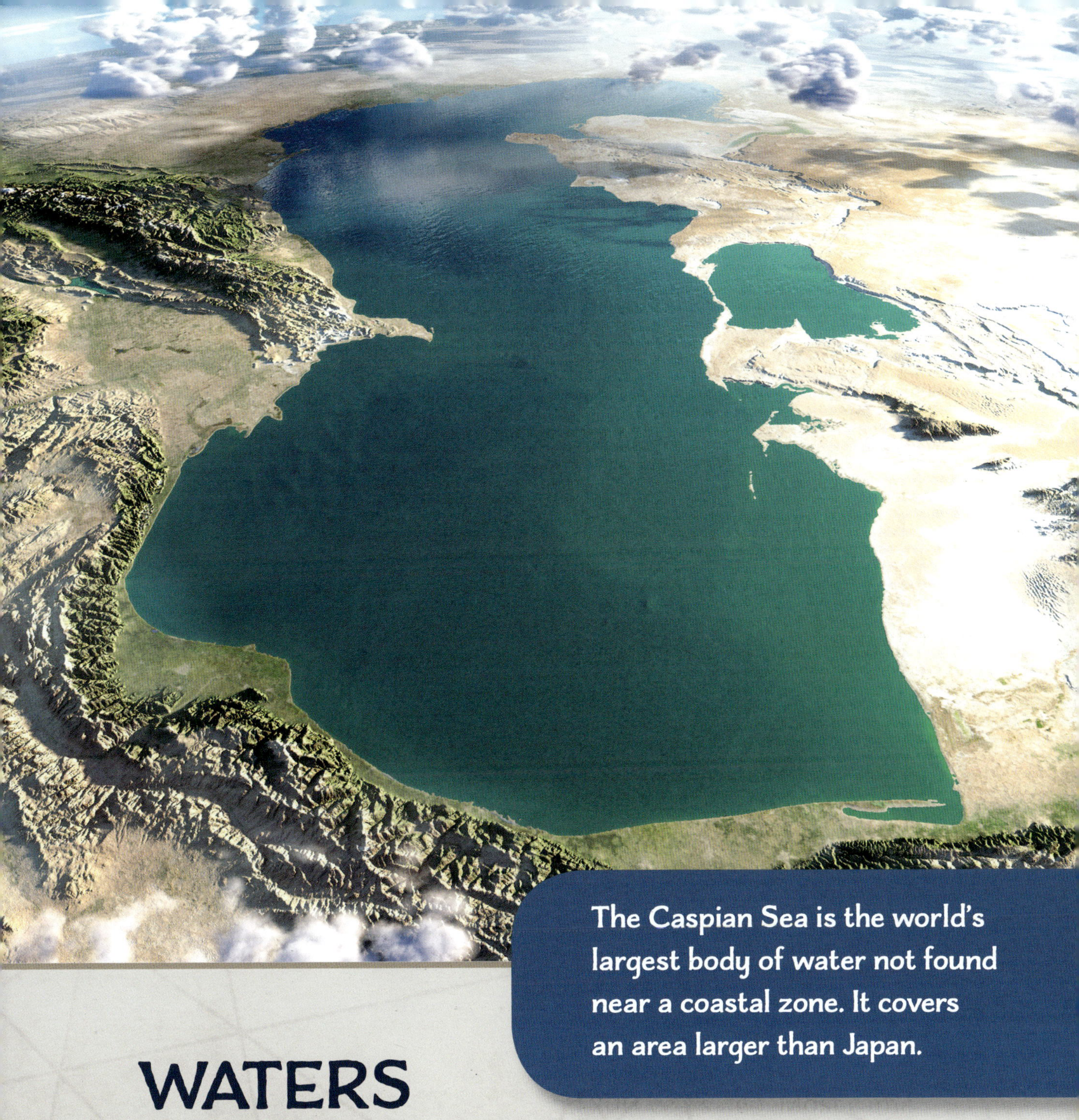

The Caspian Sea is the world's largest body of water not found near a coastal zone. It covers an area larger than Japan.

WATERS

Five main rivers flow through Europe. The Volga is the longest. It starts in Russia and empties into the Caspian Sea. The Danube is the second longest European river. It begins in Germany. The Rhine flows through western Europe, and the Elbe runs northwest. The Loire is found in France.

CLIMATE

Much of Europe is **temperate**. Western Europe is kept warm by water carried from the Gulf of Mexico by a strong ocean current. The areas near the Mediterranean Sea have hot, dry summers and mild winters.

Many tourists enjoy visiting the island of Santorini, Greece.

Northern lights glow in Norway's sky. These curtains of light happen all year, but are easier to see during the longer winter nights.

Northern Europe has a **subarctic** climate. Cold, snowy winters freeze parts of Norway, Sweden, Finland, and Russia. Summers are short and cool there. Snow and ice stay on the ground all year in some areas.

CHAPTER 3

NATURAL RESOURCES

Europe has some **minerals** useful for making goods. European feldspar is used in glass and ceramics. The continent's forests provide wood for building, paper, and fuel.

feldspar

Southern Italy has many olive trees. The olives are ground up and then pressed to squeeze out the oil.

About 39% of Europe's land is used for crops. Farmers grow grains such as wheat and barley. Grains are often sold to other countries. Cows graze on the plains and give milk. Milk can be made into butter and cheese. Some countries, such as Italy, are known for special products such as olive oil.

CHAPTER 4

PLANTS AND ANIMALS

Blackberries grow wild throughout much of Europe.

PLANTS

The first pear trees grew in southeastern Europe. Blackberries have been picked on the continent for more than 2,000 years. Snapdragon flowers are thought to have started in the western Mediterranean region.

Thick forests of trees such as elm and oak once covered much of central Europe. Over hundreds of years, people cleared trees to plant crops. They also cut them down for wood to use in homes, ships, and as fuel. Today, European countries work to replant the forests.

ANIMALS OF THE FOREST

Cutting down the forests made fewer places for bigger animals such as bears and wolves to live. But the smaller red fox **adapted** well to life around people. Today, foxes are found throughout Europe. Hedgehogs live in woods and grasslands. They also make their burrows in gardens and parks.

A red fox's hearing is so sharp that it can hear a mouse digging underground.

The Eurasian eagle owl is the largest owl in the world. They live throughout Europe and Asia.

About 400,000 moose live in the forests of Sweden. The Eurasian lynx is Europe's biggest wild cat. It was once almost wiped out. Now between 9,000 and 10,000 Eurasian lynx live in the continent's forests. Different kinds of owls also call the woods home.

ANIMALS OF THE NORTH

Caribous' thick fur protects them during harsh northern winters. Harbor seals hunt fish and shellfish along the coast. The seals' **blubber** keeps them warm in the icy water.

Harbor seals rest on rocks, beaches, and sea ice when not in the water.

Polar bears have the thickest fur of any bear.

Polar bears live on the Svalbard islands near Norway. The Svalbard polar bears were once hunted and almost wiped out. In 1973, Norway made them protected animals. Today, about 300 polar bears live in the area.

CHAPTER 5

COUNTRIES AND CITIES

Turkey is also a transcontinental country. Like Russia, Turkey is in both Europe and Asia.

Vatican City is a country inside Italy. Only about 800 people live there. Vatican City is the smallest country in the world.

COUNTRIES

Europe has 44 nations. It also has **transcontinental** countries. These countries have land in more than one continent. Most of Russia is in Asia, but some of its land is in Europe.

More Russian people make their homes in the European part of the country than in the Asian part. About 113 million Russians live in Europe. Germany is the next largest European country. More than 83 million people call Germany home. France holds about 65 million people.

CITIES

Most Europeans make their homes in towns and cities. Fewer than 30% live in the countryside. Many travelers from around the world also like to visit European cities. Some of these cities are very crowded.

The Bosphorus strait divides the European side of Istanbul from its Asian side.

St. Basil's Cathedral in Moscow, Russia, is known for its colorful domes.

Istanbul, Turkey, has land in both Europe and Asia. Istanbul is Europe's largest city. More than 15 million people live there. Moscow is in the European part of Russia. Moscow holds more than 12 million people. It is the second largest city in Europe.

CHAPTER 6

CULTURE AND PEOPLE

The ancient civilizations of Greece and Rome began in Europe. European kings and queens supported the Age of Exploration. They sent ships sailing around the world. European settlers founded colonies on nearly all of the other continents. The settlers brought their culture and languages with them.

Antarctica is the only continent with no European colonies. It was far too cold for settlers to live there.

Välkommen
dobrodošli bienvenido
Bine ati venit bem vitajte
vinda Witamy
Tere καλως
tulemast ΗΡΘΑΤΕ willkommen
Welkom Vítejte Dobrodošli
добре дошли welcome
laipni
Tervetuloa Velkommen
gaidīti
Üdvözöljük
benvenuto bienvenu
fáilte roimh chách merħba Sveiki

Europe has 24 official languages. Some people may share a language but not a country or a culture. For example, French is an official language of Switzerland. But Swiss people are not the same as those who live in France.

FOOD

European food is well-known around the world. Spaghetti and pizza began in Italy. France's grapes become wine and champagne. People everywhere enjoy England's fish and chips and Belgium's waffles.

Cricket is England's national summer sport.

SPORTS

Soccer began in Europe. It is still the most popular sport across the continent. Each country also has other favorites. The English enjoy cricket. Austrians like to ski. Ice hockey is played in Finland.

GLOSSARY

adapt (uh-DAPT): To change to be able to fit new conditions

blubber (BLUH-br): The thick layer of fat on whales, seals, and some other sea animals

border (BOR-dr): The place where one area ends and another starts

equator (EE-kway-tr): An imaginary line around the middle of Earth that is the same distance from the North Pole to the South Pole

mineral (MIH-nuh-rl): A solid substance that is formed naturally under the ground

peninsula (puh-NIN-suh-luh): A piece of land almost completely surrounded by water but is attached to a larger land area

plains (PLAYNZ): A large stretch of mostly flat land

subarctic (sub-ARK-tick): The region immediately south of the Arctic Circle

temperate (TEM-pr-uht): Neither very hot nor very cold

transcontinental (tranz-kon-ti-NEN-tuhl): Crossing a continent

INDEX

COMPREHENSION QUESTIONS

1. How many people live in Europe?

a. Fewer than 10 million

b. About 100 million

c. More than 700 million

2. Which animal lives in the European forests?

a. Moose

b. Caribou

c. Polar bear

3. Which country in Europe has the most people?

a. Russia

b. Germany

c. France

4. True or False: Europe is north of the equator.

5. True of False: More Europeans live in the countryside than in the cities.

Answers: 1. C, 2. A, 3. A, 4. True, 5. False

ABOUT THE AUTHOR

Tracy Vonder Brink loves true stories and facts. She has written more than 20 books for kids and is a contributing editor for three children's science magazines. Tracy lives in Cincinnati, Ohio, with her husband, two daughters, and two rescue dogs.

Written by: Tracy Vonder Brink
Cover design by: Kathy Walsh
Interior design by: Kathy Walsh
Series Development: James Earley
Proofreader: Crystal Sikkens
Educational Consultant: Marie Lemke M.Ed.
Print coordinator: Katherine Berti

Photographs: Shutterstock; Cover: ©Triff, ©Khurasan, ©nypl, @Dima_designer, ©Boris Stroujko; Title Pg: ©Triff, ©Dima_designer; Pg 3-31: ©Triff; Pg 4-31: ©Omeris, ©nataliya_ua; Pg 4: ©Aleksei Peretiagin; Pg 6: ©Smelov; Pg 7: ©Morphius Film; Pg 8: ©Mike Pellinni; Pg 9: © Eva Bocek; Pg 10: ©Lukasz Janyst; Pg 11: ©Anton Balazh; Pg 12: ©Patryk Kosmider; Pg 13: ©Denis Belitsky; Pg 14: ©Pogorelova, ©vvoe; Pg 15: ©Deyan Georgiev, Sabina Berezina; Pg 16: ©Just Life; Pg 17: ©GuilhermeSoares, ©EllSan; Pg 18: ©Ondrej Prosicky; Pg 19: ©duangnapa_b; Pg 20: ©Sharp Photography @Wiki; Pg 21: ©Chase Dekker; Pg 22: © Pyty; Pg 23: ©ESB Professional; Pg 24: ©Seqoya; Pg 25: ©Baturina Yuliya; Pg 26: ©iurii; Pg 27: ©Ben Gingell, © Anastasia Boiko, ©Filip Bjorkman; Pg 28: ©Brent Hofacker; Pg 29: ©Philip Bird LRPS CPAGB

Library and Archives Canada Cataloguing in Publication

Available at the Library and Archives Canada

Library of Congress Cataloging-in-Publication Data

Available at the Library of Congress

Crabtree Publishing Company

www.crabtreebooks.com 1-800-387-7650

In Canada: We acknowledge the financial support of the Government of Canada through the Canada Book Fund for our publishing activities.

Published in the United States
Crabtree Publishing
347 Fifth Avenue
Suite 1402-145
New York, NY, 10016

Published in Canada
Crabtree Publishing
616 Welland Ave.
St. Catharines, ON
L2M 5V6

Printed in the U.S.A./072022/CG20220201